THE CONNECTICUT RIVER

The Connecticut River

Photographs by WILLIAM F. STEKL

Text by EVAN HILL

Introduction by ROGER TORY PETERSON

Foreword by ABE RIBICOFF

WESLEYAN UNIVERSITY PRESS   Middletown, Connecticut

Library of Congress Cataloging in
Publication Data

Stekl, William F.
      The Connecticut River.

        1. Connecticut River. I. Hill, Evan.
II. Title.
F12.C7S8   917.4'04'40222   72-3727
ISBN 0-8195-4051-X

Published in cooperation with the Middletown Press Publishing Company

MANUFACTURED IN THE UNITED STATES OF AMERICA

FIRST EDITION

Contents

Photographs

Introduction

A river has many faces and can be made to serve many purposes. You can drink it or bathe in it; use its surface as a highway for cargo carriers or pleasure craft; dam it for flood control or irrigation or power; cross it with bridges or let it remain as a barrier to land travel; pollute it with sewage, chemical runoff, and industrial waste or preserve it in life-giving ecological balance. And if the river is as varied and beautiful as the Connecticut, you can merely look at it — in the long light of a sultry summer evening, under an angry winter sky, in the high color of autumn or the pastel shades of spring — and derive that sense of peace and uplift of the spirit that most men find in living water.

In these pages, Mr. Stekl with his camera and Mr. Hill with his informed and perceptive observations take you on a guided tour of the Connecticut River — in space, from mouth to source; in time, back to the first settlements and beyond, forward a step or two into a problematical tomorrow. This is a river whose banks have supported aboriginal man for millennia and civilized man for more than three centuries. Its waters have been navigated; its fishes harvested; farms and towns and factories have proliferated along its shores; dams and bridges have been built.

Yet, despite continuing use and a certain amount of abuse, the river in much of its aspect remains remarkably unspoiled, as these magnificent photographs will show.

For those who know and love this river, there is recognition here, perhaps nostalgia. For those who do not, there is discovery. Some of what you will find in these pages is sheer pastoral beauty. Some of it is more than a little shocking in its revelation of human heedlessness and irresponsibility — for although a very beautiful river, it is also a troubled river that cries out for a healing hand.

All of it, too, underlines the need to save our river while we can. At the turn of the century, when our nation supported some seventy-six million people, the states through which the Connecticut flows had about four million and a half; and there were no expressways pouring urban swarms into the open country. Today, the population figures have more than doubled; cars and concrete have become new environmental factors. But in the face of this ever-growing pressure the area of the Connecticut Valley has increased not at all. The point needs no belaboring.

Is the Connecticut worth saving? Look at these photographs, read this text, and make your own judgment. I need not offer an opinion. I need only mention that I have seen rather more of the world's surface than most men ever do, and I have chosen the valley of this river for my home.

ROGER TORY PETERSON

Old Lyme, Connecticut
March 1972

Foreword

This book is a tribute to the beauty of the Connecticut River. I hope it does not become an elegy as well, for the threats to the river increase every year.

The Connecticut River has never experienced the intensive development common to most major waterways, in part because a sandbar at its mouth has always prohibited the entrance of deep-draft vessels. As a result, long stretches of the river's 400-mile shoreline remain relatively untouched by modern America.

Flowing through the center of historic New England, and in part surrounded by a great urban sprawl, the Connecticut River provides an unmatched array of the vital natural beauties which are fast disappearing in our urbanized society. The preservation and renewal of these assets is of great importance, not only to Connecticut and the other states through which the river passes but to the entire nation.

Ironically, for years the poor water quality of the Connecticut River limited residential construction along its banks. The enactment of federal pollution-control laws and the purification of the water, however, mean that the untouched areas will be ripe for development. Unless action is taken to prevent it, the riverbank from Long Island Sound to the Canadian border will be covered with manufacturing plants, shopping centers, housing tracts, and marinas.

In an attempt to prevent further degradation of the river, I introduced legislation in 1966 authorizing a comprehensive study of its valley. The resulting report recommended that the federal government act to preserve three of the most valuable sections of the river: the Coos region near the Canadian border; the Mount Holyoke region in Massachusetts; and the Gateway area of southern Connecticut. The Senate has unanimously approved my subsequent bill creating a Connecticut Historic Riverway in the Gateway area between East Haddam and Old Saybrook; at this writing, the House has yet to act on it.

The Historic Riverway will be unlike any other national park. It is based on the concept that the nature of the resource should dictate its best use. Everyone interested in the river agrees that neither the land nor the local life style could survive intensive development. As a result, the legislation emphasizes the preservation of the physical and social environment of the area. Much of the present land use would be frozen, and local citizens would participate in the development and administration of the national park.

Time is running out for the Connecticut River. It would be sad to see a valley which survived man's ravages for over three hundred years destroyed just when the nation is waking up to the many threats faced by our natural resources.

ABE RIBICOFF

United States Senate
Washington, D.C.
April 1972

12

THE CONNECTICUT RIVER

As New England rivers flow, the Connecticut is long — 410 miles from the sandbar at its wide mouth on salt Long Island Sound to the sweet, small springs that spawn it in New Hampshire hills a few hundred yards from Canada.

In that length it drops 2200 feet, from glittering frivolity in its upper reaches, through roaring power at its falls, to swollen lassitude in its lower tidal stretch.

The Hudson is about 100 miles shorter; the Housatonic and the Merrimack, the Aroostook and the Kennebec — all touched with the mighty music of Indian names as is the Connecticut — are each about a third as long. In Algonkian the Connecticut is the Kwinitekwa or the Quinnehtukgut or the Quan-eh-ta-kut, depending on the phonics of the English transcriber. It means Long River, as Kwini-beke (Kennebec) meant Long Lake to the Algonkians who paddled both. A 1688 French map calls it the Conitic.

An earlier Dutch map calls it the Versche (Fresh) River and it flows through a land called Connitekock, past Weeters Velt (Wethersfield) and Voynser (Windsor) and Herfort (Hartford). Farther south are the early towns of Gilfort, Milfort, Nieu-haven, and Stamfort.

The Dutch had second choice to name it, for they were the Europeans to find it and chart it, and their name for it was as simple and as accurate as was the Indian name that has endured.

It is tempting to think of a river as beginning at its source, with the first pure sparkling droplet dangling from the needle of a spruce, then merging with another until the drops become a seep and the seep becomes a trickle. Two trickles join to vein a sloping meadow, and inexorably a million, billion droplets weld into a mighty stream sweeping to an ocean to evaporate in particles and complete the grand circle of nature — to again become a sun-distilled, crystal droplet on a spruce.

The Connecticut can be traced this way — from the bubble foam of Scott's bog water dimpling through the four small New Hampshire lakes that bear its name, tumbling into Pittsburg already dropped down 800 feet in less than thirty miles and rushing farther south. Joined by icy water from the Presidential Range, thawed from snow peaked high on Washington and Madison and Adams. Joined by the Nulhegan from Vermont and the Ottoqueechee and the White and Black — more

Looking landward from the Sound

than 13,000 square miles to drain in its full length — and swelled still more by the Wild Ammonoosuc, the Mascoma, the Sugar, the Ashuelot.

In late winter it swells sullenly beneath its blackening ice, chained by temperature. Then the warming earth disintegrates its rotting crystal sheath and releases it to roar with new life past a thousand New England doors, surging sparkling into spring.

Downstream, downstream, led inconstantly by constant gravity, over dams, gnawing at the Hartland rapids, hissing at the rocks of Bellows Falls, nibbling softly at canals built to tame it.

To Mount Tom in Massachusetts where the huge long-log drives of pine and spruce were yarded in the Great Oxbow until sawyers could rip them into planks and boards and beams.

Past Holyoke, the user of the river, past Springfield where its use is nearly gone. Over Turner's Falls and then miles of meanders through fine farming land, spreading, in flood time, rich New Hampshire loam floated a hundred miles downstream.

Past Warehouse Point where in 1635 a hard-headed Puritan fur trader named William Pynchon watched Indians unload their canoes at a point on the river and then he built a warehouse there — a spot to be forever named after the building rather than its builder.

Then past Hartford and Middletown and the Portland brownstone quarries; past Higganum and Hamburg Cove and brackish water now for the sea's tide sweeps up as far as sixty miles from Long Island Sound, and then the salt and the beach and the spot in Old Saybrook where Yale could not be kept and the sandstone slab on legs that marks the 1644 grave of Lady Alice Fenwick — the lady with the golden hair — and here the river ends, its bite diminished, its pure upstate New England waters diluted in the sea, unrecognizable, undistinguished, ended.

Yet a river really begins at its mouth, where most often man discovers it. Here it is most powerful, filled with the collection of its fluid capital, the accumulated banking of its watershed.

Upstream it dwindles into childhood, sometimes into senile childhood as its

Old Saybrook, Connecticut, Lynde Light

banks close in and its volume and its strength decrease but its beauty and caprice increase.

A river is obedient water carving contours until people gather there. And people always do. Still water has a limpid fascination, but moving water is mesmerizing to man. He must touch and fondle it, divert it, control it. It is not only that he must drink it or die, it is that he must feel it or his heart will wither.

When the Connecticut was first found by Europeans, the water was high. It was in either April or May of 1614, the flood time of the year when it holds about 150 times its average volume, and as much as 800 times its midsummer minimum. Water, muddy with early spring runoff and rushing floating debris to the sea, ran high on the lower banks.

Its discoverer, Adriaen Block, was a Dutch fur trader and explorer, who had arrived in New Netherlands from Holland just five years after Hudson found the Hudson, and who was to pick up a cargo of Indian-trapped furs for the Dutch East India Company. But his ship burned to the waterline before he could sail. So he and his crew pegged together another ship — a 16-ton, 44-foot-long sloop with a single sail — and named it the *Onrust (Restless)*.

He pointed it east to probe the unknown shape of Long Island Sound. He explored the mouth of the Housatonic near what is now Bridgeport, then coasted east to the wide, shallow mouth of the Connecticut. In the high water he slid over the sandbar at its mouth. (It is this sandbar that has preserved Old Lyme and Old Saybrook as picturesque rural villages.)

He sailed upstream as far as the Enfield Falls, which stopped him sixty-nine miles from the Sound. And by now he knew the wide, winding strip of water was indeed a river. Its speed had steadily increased, the tides had diminished, and the water no longer was brackish. He named it the Fresh Water River.

He sailed to the mouth again, past the coves and marshes, and turned east. He found Block Island which is named for him and went on to Cape Cod for further exploration. There he left the *Restless*, boarded another vessel, and shipped home on it, arriving there in July.

And the river had begun, for now Europeans knew of it.

18

Old Saybrook, wetlands

A sandbar at its mouth has left the Connecticut the only major river in the nation without a city at its mouth. Instead there are twin villages, quiet even with the summer people, and one of them was named Saybrook in 1635 by an English company of colonists; they were honoring Lord Say and Lord Brooke, the company's major proprietors, who never saw the land that still bears their names three centuries later.

The other, Old Lyme, contains Great Island, rich with marsh grasses, seaside goldenrod, glasswort, sea lavender, and water hemp. Here is where the osprey nest high above the beach's soft-shell clams and oysters, sharing levels of their airspace with turkey buzzards, waterfowl, and gulls.

Yale College, third oldest in the nation, was founded at Old Saybrook in 1701 and called "The Collegiate School," but didn't last there long. After fifteen years of what they considered intolerable isolation at the mouth of the river, college officials selected New Haven as their home. But Saybrookers did not take the move with any sense of graciousness. They stood defiantly in the doorway of the library to prevent the books from being carted off; they cut loose the horses from the movers' wagons; they demolished small bridges and ripped the planking off larger ones on the route to New Haven. But it did no good. Today all that remains of Yale is a bronze marker that says it once was there.

Essex, South Cove

Not long ago Saybrook and Lyme and Deep River and Essex were places you went to on a Sunday trip from Hartford. Now they're places you live in and leave to go to work in Hartford; Essex is now one of the most active yachting centers on the East Coast.

In fact, the old roads south from Hartford left the river there, allowing it to remain tranquil in neglect. They swept southwest to where the business was — to New Haven and New York — and the sedate dignity of the lower valley was preserved. But today that pattern is changed, with wide, fast highways shooting nearly straight from Middletown to Saybrook.

22

Essex, from the air

With one of the finest harbors on the East Coast, Essex has been in the ship-building business since it began, about 1675, peopled by wanderers from downstream Saybrook. The first U.S. warship, the 24-gun *Oliver Cromwell*, was launched there in time for the Revolution.

By 1814 it was important enough to invite a raid by British marines slashing at the American coast during the War of 1812. The shipyards in the Middle and North Coves were burned and the loss of vessels ranged from twenty-two to forty, depending on the historian. Essex itself settles for twenty-eight, a number sufficiently impressive to document the importance of the town.

Its coves are some of the most beautiful on the river; its homes, many of them built by sea captains, among the nation's best designed.

BRITISH MARINES
LANDED HERE AND BURNED
28 LOCAL SHIPS
APRIL 8 1814

About one-half mile wide at its mouth, about three miles long, and the beginning of the Eightmile River, Hamburg Cove has been known to man since man has known it as one of the prettiest spots on the Connecticut.

Wandering sturgeon the size of porpoises cruise its length; for years boatmen have sailed softly into its shelter to anchor overnight and absorb its quietness and beauty.

Aspen, birch, and even yet some surviving elm that so far have escaped the Dutch disease that kills them, feed along the river bank near luscious global maples.

In 1817 the Boston Transcript described it as " . . . an earthly paradise. Broadening a bit as you ascend it, the waters are covered with a luxuriant mass of wild rice. Cardinal Flower . . . grow along the margin of the water in a passionate splendor of color."

The description is accurate fifteen decades later. There is still wild rice luxuriant, and in the autumn the shore's edge is dotted with tall red gladioluslike blooms, waving in the wind on their wheat-stem stalks.

Hamburg Cove

Deep River, backwater

Almost everywhere there is fecund beauty; musty, spermy, bursting spring. High water; higher spirits and a drive for life; unfolding buds and leaves and loss of winter tempers.

A scintilla of sunbeam. A pollen mote. A bird's clear cry. And always the steady, softly hissing presence of the river.

It's so fine you want to buy it all and fence it in to keep it clean and lovely and invite the world to come and look and love it too. But please keep off the grass, and don't peel the paper birch or dump your beer cans here, and don't spray-paint your initials on the gray-green lichen or the ancient glacier-carried granite boulders. Don't. But we have.

Deep River, navigation marker

Chester

Once this ferry from Chester to Hadlyme was a sailboat owned by a man whose father had given it to him as a wedding gift, with the sensible Yankee proviso that all tolls more than $30 a year would go to Dad. A man wishing to cross blew a horn hanging from a maple near the landing. Today, from the terrace at Gillette's Castle, the blunt ferry resembles a wooden toy sawed from a pine 2 x 4 for a muddy boy to send floating down a melted gutter stream in spring, and its distance-muted engines gently send their cushioned putta-ta-putta-ta probing to the river's bank.

Gillette's Castle itself, hanging above the river on a craggy bank, is a mason's cobbled monster, architecturally unbelievable. But its builder, Hartford-born William Gillette, one of the nation's best-known actors in the early twentieth century, can be forgiven his eccentric architectural taste. The site for his castle is magnificent. Gillette piled glacier-rounded stone on glacier-rounded stone and buttered them with mortar and cobbled nearly everything to which cement would stick. But he didn't alter nature.

In his will he ordered his executors to be sure that the property did not get into "the possession of some blithering saphead who has no conception of where he is or with what surrounded."

Six years after his death in 1937 at eighty-two years of age, his executors obeyed his blistering order. The State of Connecticut got the castle and its 158 acres and 3200 feet of river frontage, and nearly 150,000 visitors each year picnic there and share the view he preserved for them.

Gillette's Castle, picnic tables

Hadlyme

It was so decrepit then, so close to the smash of a wrecker's ball swung lazily, that it was not even mentioned in the 1938 WPA Guide to Connecticut.

Five years later, greasy, mud-splashed state highway trucks rumbled in and out, splattering its pure Victorian architecture with oil, after men had ripped off its graceful balconies and porches. It became a state warehouse, unpainted, unrepaired, neglected, soon to be condemned.

Yet for nearly thirty years after it opened in 1877, the Goodspeed Opera House — originally called Goodspeed's Hall — had been the architectural gem of the Connecticut River. Six stories high, with its top two stories devoted to a graceful Baroque theatre, seating more than three hundred on its main floor and in its gently sweeping horseshoe balcony and stage-side boxes, it brought complete stage companies, and patrons too, upstream from New York City. Often they arrived on William Goodspeed's riverboats, to land at Goodspeed's Landing, to stay at Goodspeed's hotel, eat at his restaurant, ride across the river (if they wished) on Goodspeed's ferry (there was no bridge there then) named the *Goodspeed*, and cash their checks at Goodspeed's bank, which along with his general store occupied the first three floors of the building. The fourth floor was rented out as office space.

Goodspeed's death robbed the building of its most successful promoter, and then the decline of the riverboat brought on the fast decline of the Goodspeed.

By 1920, the Opera House (then owned by the New Haven Railroad, which Goodspeed had helped to form) had played to its last audience. Railroads are not known for successful theatre, although a World War I militia unit had lived in the building while guarding the Haddam bridge from possible sabotage by German submarines.

Forty years later the building tottered on the river's edge, doomed by the state of Connecticut which had bought it and four acres of river land in 1943 for $4,000. But now it was clearly unsafe for any use. A contract for its demolition was ready for signature.

Then the Goodspeed Opera House Foundation, a non-profit, charitable group which still owns and operates it, rescued it. They paid the state one dollar

Goodspeed Opera House, East Haddam Landing

for the building, then sunk nearly three-quarters of a million more dollars into restoring it.

It reopened in 1963 with a Jerome Kern musical.

In 1965 *Man of La Mancha* had its world premiere on Mr. Goodspeed's stage, before moving on to New Haven, New York, and around the world. Today private parties come up the river again from New York City, following the course of theatre-goers nearly a century ago. It is not uncommon to see a 100-foot ocean-going yacht tied up at Goodspeed's old landing, with a party of thirty-five ashore. Goodspeed's bank is closed, and his general store is gone. His opera house, however, is often full.

In January the river's ice seeps down, making crystals, sheets, then floes of ice as far south as Haddam, thickening to near-molasses until the tiny snappling crack that turns moving slush to solid ice.

Then Coast Guard cutters surge upstream, cleaving strongly, splitting the ice so that cargo can reach as far upstream as Hartford.

The mouth of Salmon River, from the air

The brine tang of the tide diminishes, diluted by hardwood winds, dissolved in the rolling fresh water pouring from the north.

The riverscape is unbelievably restful, soft, flowing as gently as the waters. Lawns and bay and marsh and deciduous trees sweep to the river's edge and send down roots to suck up soil-filtered waters.

Occasionally a white colonial house is seen, near or on a high flood-safe bank, but those are few. There is no strangling necklace of wooden-cottage-beads along this shore, as there is on lakes and ponds and other streams and upon Long Island Sound itself. Not yet.

A cruising herring gull skims down as if to lap the water. A small V-convoy of ducks flaps lustily along — as purposeful on compass course as the gull is purposeless in his.

The riverboat *Dolly Madison*

Valley residents are split on the Yankee Atomic Power plant at Haddam Neck. Some call it a pregnant barn; others see some pleasant form, if not pure beauty, in its shape as they cruise past it on a riverboat.

Some fear the heat it pours into the river, feeling sure that it is harmful to aquatic life. They want the plant shut down, or forced to chill its discharge water; they also want no more atomic plants on this river or on others or just anywhere. Others say its half-million kilowatts of electricity production is needed badly, that power has precedence over fish.

Every minute that it operates the Haddam plant sucks up more than a third of a million gallons of Connecticut River water. It needs that water to cool its innards. It could cool itself by other means — by evaporating towers that would also fog the landscape, create artificial rain and snow for several square miles, and cost perhaps a hundred million dollars.

But the river is less costly, and more efficient. Its temperature, even in the hottest months, is cool enough to be effective. Thus it swirls through the Haddam plant to wash the heat from nuclear devices, and by cooling, warms itself. And thus each minute nearly one-third of a million gallons of the Connecticut River, borrowed and diverted and made warmer, is discharged back. And now its temperature is as high as 93 degrees, considerably warmer than the rest of the river.

What harm does it do? According to John R. Clark in *Scientific American*, 93 degrees Fahrenheit is essentially uninhabitable for all U.S. fish except certain southern species. Higher than normal temperatures cause fish to need more oxygen, and there is less oxygen in warmer water; warmer water makes fish metabolism race; it makes fish grow faster, die sooner. It also attracts fish, as sports fishermen well know. And in 1968 many menhaden were killed in the Cape Cod Canal when they got trapped in the 93-degree discharge from a power plant.

Yet, so far, fears of wide-spread destructive thermal pollution on the Connecticut near Haddam seem unjustified, although fish larvae sucked through the plant have died. A five-year, $700,000 study of the thermal effect of Yankee Atomic, conducted by the Connecticut State Water Resources Commission, has found little harm to the river's aquatic life, to either fish or bottom organisms. The study, per-

Yankee Atomic power plant, Haddam Neck

formed by university scientists, found that perch and catfish are attracted to warmer water until it hits 96 degrees, when they scoot off for cooler spots. Shad, some of which had sound transmitters implanted in their stomachs for the study, have been tracked for miles from well below to well above the Haddam plant, and they seem unaffected by the flume of warmer water reaching out into the river. The heat has increased the supply of marine food in the area, but two miles downstream from the plant, the river is back to normal temperature.

Even so, the fears of thermal pollution have been productive. We now have more knowledge about the effects of heat on marine life, and we can protect our rivers and our fish more effectively with the muscle that knowledge gives us.

45

The Haddams love their river so much that they straddle it with dumps (they set fire to them and manufactured airborne stench until 1970), making to it weekly offerings of life's left-overs — dead animals and stones and leafmold scraped from around their houses, bottles and broken glass and crockery and cans of thickened paint and whiskey flasks not quite emptied on a Saturday night; excreted paper diapers and used-up rubber controls for body, birth, and life and death; metal, plastic, cloth, and wood — a midden heap of hopes and plans forsaken. And they leave it near the river. When high water comes the river seeps up to it, tasting, touching, gathering some contemporary artifacts and distributing them downstream to merge with sand and salt and the chemicals of man and nature, to become in some far distant unnamed geologic age the fossils and the signs of what man once did to and with himself and what he loved.

46

A quiet backwater on the lower river

Somewhere not far from where this white swan cruises in the placid backwash of the river at East Haddam there was, about twenty thousand years ago, a great dam built by the last receding glacier.

Hurd Park, near Middle Haddam

As the glacier retreated north, shrinking snakelike up the valley, it dropped what it had earlier stripped away from farther north, from the White Mountains of New Hampshire, from the Green Mountains of Vermont. These gougings of gravel, sand, and giant boulders were sometimes dropped in heaps.

The heap at East Haddam straddled the river and backed up the melting glacier's water as far north as Lyme, New Hampshire, 157 miles upstream. But it could not contain that prehistoric lake. Water gushed over the top of it in a fall as great as or greater than Niagara.

And then one day, in one cataclysmic gasp, it collapsed and the giant lake rushed to Long Island Sound, an enormous flood of water suddenly released. Where it had been, there grew the Connecticut River. And on its banks, in what is now Massachusetts and Connecticut, were left the broad, thick layers of glacial silt, the rich lake bottom that seeded itself to forest and was later seeded by man.

Mesozoic tremblers of the steaming prehistoric swamps — megalosaurus, iguanodon, tyrannosaurus rex — mashed along with fernlike fronds of giant conifers in an early recycling of matter; from living animal and plant to carbon, coal with fossil imprints of its living source. Then to ugly heaps like this one piled near Middletown by the Hartford Electric Light Company, so close to the edge of the Connecticut that its blackness, soon to be flame and smoke and electric power, can easily be seen from the surface of the river.

And downstream only a few miles is the clean, gleaming dome of Yankee Atomic, a much less ancient, more esthetically tolerable source of energy, powered by the atom.

Fossil fuel for electric power, near Middletown

The Indians first used the river for transportation. Their canoes and dugouts traveled up and down it, the Agawams, the Podunks, Sicaogs, trading with the downstream Wangunks and the Hammonassets, hunting, trapping, fishing.

Adriaen Block bought beaver in 1614 from Indians who delivered the pelts in canoes. In September 1633 what was probably the continent's first prefabricated building — manufactured by the colonists in Plymouth on Cape Cod — was transported up the river, brought ashore and quickly erected against the coming winter, and the town of Windsor was founded.

Then came the sloops and schooners and the brigs in the West Indies trade, sometimes taking two weeks to sail upriver to Hartford from Saybrook — as long as the trip from the Caribbean to the river's mouth. Then flatboats, taking cargo north from Hartford, poled through the rapids and against the stream by hard-drinking, hard-living brutes of men.

Farther north the river became a giant's sluice each spring at break-up time. For then, while high water lasted, up-country loggers dumped into it millions of long logs cut in New Hampshire and Vermont, and the river carried them to sawmills, some as far south as the Great Oxbow at Mount Tom, Massachusetts.

Thirty sandbars thwart the river, and the shipper, between Hartford and the Sound, but the river is still used heavily. More than three million tons of cargo are shipped up it each year. More than half of it is fuel oil, carried in tankers like this one at the right, which is heading downstream empty.

52

Middletown

Middletown is on the west bank; Portland, once called East Middletown, is on the east. Both were settled in the middle of the seventeenth century by wandering Puritans who floated down from the upriver towns of Wethersfield and Hartford.

For half a century after 1750 Middletown, named because it sits halfway between the river's mouth and the northern head of navigation, was the state's largest and wealthiest town. Charles Dickens, not always taken with things American, called its High Street "the most beautiful street in America."

Portland, beginning in the middle 1600's and continuing until recent years, has quarried and shipped throughout the world enormous quantities of Connecticut brownstone. Huge barges floated it downriver on the way to Manhattan, where the famous New York brownstone houses were built of it, especially during the late nineteenth century when the Portland quarries employed 850 men, 200 oxen, and 60 horses.

Fossil tracks of dinosaurs, who slogged through the valley in the Mesozoic Era of geologic time (perhaps a hundred million years ago, give or take ten million years or so) and left their footprints in early Connecticut river mud, long before the glacier dammed it shut, are common in the quarries.

Middletown, River Road

Common too is modern man's domestic refuse, abandoned, rotting, on the river's shore.

Near Gildersleeve Island, above the city of Middletown, the tranquility is so reassuring, the rush of restfulness so kind, so cotton-batting mind-relaxing, that you forgive even the giant clumsy coal pile downstream. You realize that it really does not rupture the eyes or ruin the rapture.

Already you have pardoned the Baldwin Bridge slicing across the river's mouth, clean, but coarse and graceless in its function. You know that rivers must be spanned, and the Baldwin's steel and concrete are so much less offensive than the ugly, rusting, rotting spans of railroad bridges. You know that a lovely wooden covered bridge, like those at Windsor, Vermont, or at Lancaster, New Hampshire, is really too much to ask.

But the vertically corrugated ugly marinas — those metallic, graceless "yacht basins" are unforgiveable — as abrasive to the senses as the filth of feces and toilet paper tumbling into the river upstream at Springfield, Massachusetts.

Then quietly, her blue hull hissing past you and her white sails bellied pregnantly, the MS 2607K glides towards the river's mouth and you wave back at graceful, pink-cheeked teenagers grinning, and your heart lifts, balanced now between what is and what must and soon will be.

You, too, have licked the crisp salt winds of Old Lyme and Saybrook from your lips as you know they will after a couple of hour's sail to the south, and your worry over the pollution problem is diluted temporarily.

And it is comforting to know that Middletown, for nearly fifty years one of the busiest ports on the continent, which in the nineteenth century shipped out more tonnage than New York, now has its river wharf planted to grass that needs mowing like a public park, that its single bulbous great cast-iron bollard is rusty because so very few hawsers now slip over it to hold boats fast against the river's sluggish tug, and that a fat, blue-uniformed policeman drags in the lead line and the heavy hawser when occasionally the excursion boat *Dolly Madison* comes in for a landing.

56

Beginning with Middletown and continuing north through Hartford, past the Springfield-Holyoke blemish, a few cities cluster on the river, some drawing from it, all draining into it.

But when you pass Bellows Falls in Vermont, itself an architectural discomfort leaning against the river bank in awkard red brick solemness, the river is pretty much the river that was — as it is below Middletown. It's not quite as sweet as when Timothy Dwight cruised it at the turn of the nineteenth century and praised the "purity, salubrity, and sweetness of its waters," but it now is nearly so in stretches, and it will be again, in time, for its full length.

As early as 1884 conservationists were warning about what cities do to rivers. A Manchester, Connecticut, resident angrily wrote: "A land with its rivers running filth instead of pure water, is like a body with its veins running filth instead of pure blood . . . Hartford sits nervously in the lap of what was once one of the fairest and sweetest, and now is one of the filthiest valleys in the world."

An indignant writer is often guilty of exaggeration, for certainly the Connecticut River valley was not then — and is not now, when conditions along it are even worse — one of the filthiest in the world. But, eight years before this man wrote those words, the city of Hartford was drinking Connecticut River water. In 1855 a huge 250-horsepower steam engine powered a pump to lift the river's water to a reservoir on Lord's Hill in Hartford. But by 1876 the river was too polluted by upstream dumping, and instead of forming a river compact and cleaning up its waters, the city changed its source and left the clean-up for later generations, who have yet to bring the river back to what it was in 1855.

Since before Colonial times the valley has been plagued by flood. In later years, dams on the river's tributaries have lessened danger, but before these there were periodic disasters. In 1826, 1840, 1862 the river rampaged. Again in 1927, this time as late as November.

But the highest flood was in March of 1936, when four feet of snow in the mountains of New Hampshire and Vermont were cut to one-fourth that depth in less than four days by heavy rain and warm temperatures. Millions of dollars of damage was done throughout the length of the river, and in Hartford the river rose more than thirty-seven feet above its normal level.

Since then the Army Corps of Engineers, the states themselves, and the power companies control the river's tantrums. But even so, each spring East Hartford can expect some temporary flooding as the ice melts far upstream.

There is a wonderful story — too bad that it's apocryphal — about salmon being so plentiful in the Connecticut in colonial times that indentured servants coming from England to the colonies along the river insisted that their masters agree in writing not to feed them salmon more than three times a week.

Then there is the one about salmon running so heavily at the mouth that a man could strap on his snowshoes and cross the Connecticut from Old Saybrook to Old Lyme by walking across the backs of the fish swarming upstream to their spawning grounds.

And once there was a single haul of 3,700 salmon off the mouth, the stories say.

What magnificent scenes to show how rich the river was in fish!

But common sense as well as historical and scientific knowledge rip huge rents in the tales, especially in the absence of documentation.

Salmon in England was a great luxury, afforded only by the very rich. What commoner would demand in writing that he not be fed the equivalent of steak three times a week? More likely he would be delighted at such a stroke of luck.

Then the science. Fish biologists point out that, unlike Pacific salmon which do indeed run so heavily at spawning time that they can jam a river's mouth, the Atlantic salmon run from ice-out in the spring until October or November, with hardly any entering the mouth of the Connecticut during the months of June, July, August, or September when the normal temperature of the lower river is in the low 80's, too hot for salmon. Then, too, the mouth of the Connecticut is at the southern limit of the Atlantic salmon's range, and almost never does any fish or mammal concentrate in large numbers at the limit of its range.

Most probably the fish that was scorned by indentured servants was the one scorned by nearly everyone along the river during Colonial times — the shad. Because they were so plentiful, glutting the rivers during their runs from early April into July, but heaviest in May and June, ranging up to Bellows Falls, Vermont, where the

raging water dropped near-vertical to stop them — because they were so plentiful, any colonist known to eat them was considered too poor to be able to afford pork, and was socially bankrupt. Shad-eating became reputable only about thirty years before the Revolution, and then the fish were packed into barrels for soldiers' rations, a quartermaster decision that probably did not enhance the shad's reputation.

But it was not pollution that killed off the salmon in the river, or reduced the run of shad. It was the dams that kept them from their spawning grounds. One was built at Turner's Falls, Massachusetts, in 1798, and by 1814 salmon runs had stopped.

The Windsor Locks canal was dug out of the west bank of the Connecticut just below the Enfield dam at a time when it was taken for granted that waterways would forever be the cheapest form of transportation, and that the Connecticut River would be the major shipping artery of New England.

It made sense at the time, and four hundred Irishmen were equipped with pick and shovel to hack out a 70–foot-wide ditch that for six miles hugged the river, following its contours, avoiding the ragged water of the Enfield Rapids, and thus eliminating miles of costly portage.

The day the canal's four locks were officially completed, on November 11, 1829, fifteen boats went through them, paying tolls of $1 a passenger and 50 cents a ton for freight. It was much less expensive than the system used the day before — this involved a sailing ship to Hartford, flatboats of 10 to 18 tons to Warehouse Point in East Windsor, then oxcart around the Enfield Rapids, then back to flatboats to Springfield, Massachusetts. On downstream runs, the flatboats ran the rapids.

There were plans to dig canals around all the river's rapids. The Bellows Falls canal with its nine locks had been operating for more than twenty-five years by then, and euphoric optimists foresaw regular river shipping up as far as Barnet, Vermont, at the foot of Fifteen-Mile Falls, more than three hundred miles from the river's mouth.

But by 1850 the railroad had changed all that. The canal dams were used for water power only. Only a few river freighters needed the canals. The Windsor Locks Canal, however, never did go out of business. It is used today by pleasure boats cruising up and down the river. Each fall, like south-migrating geese that leave before freeze-up, they flock together into coveys of eight or nine and take the locks together.

About two decades after the Windsor Locks began to lift river traffic past the rapids, some Boston entrepreneurs raised $75,000 to build a power dam upstream at Holyoke, just above the Hadley Falls. Their engineers had marvelous plans for use of water power, and their new dam was to be much larger than an earlier one that was built in 1828 and had spanned the river for a short time.

But the engineers had miscalculated slightly, and on the day that the dam

Windsor Locks and Enfield Dam, from the air

was filled, these four frugal telegrams to the Boston owners told the costly five-hour story:

> 10 A.M. – Gates just closed; water filling behind dam.
>
> 12 M. – Dam leaking badly.
>
> 2 P.M. – Stones of bulk-head giving way to pressure.
>
> 3:20 P.M. – Your old dam's gone to hell by way of Willimansett.

Willimansett Rapids was downstream about a mile, and it was the last time a dam shot those rapids. A year later a replacement for the Holyoke dam, twice as costly, was completed and lasted for fifty years before being replaced.

Today the river is dammed in sixteen spots — once in Connecticut at Windsor Locks, twice in Massachusetts (one still at the site of the Holyoke leaker and one at Turner's Falls) and at thirteen spots in New Hampshire. All but one of the New Hampshire dams are owned by power and paper companies; that one — at Pittsburg — is owned by the state.

Early in 1842 Charles Dickens, visiting the United States and doing research for his *American Notes*, rode this section of the Connecticut on the twenty-five-mile journey from Springfield to Hartford.

He was a passenger on the *Massachusetts*, a boat he described as having "half a pony power" and which was too large to fit into the Windsor Locks. But, with enough water, it could shoot the Enfield Rapids. The fare was $2 for a round trip.

While Dickens made notes to describe nineteenth-century Americans, one of the boatmen watching the author noted that Dickens, "the light-weight Englishman, wore a swallow-tail snuff-colored coat, short red and white figured vest that was not long enough to reach his pantaloons, which latter were of the true Yankee check and looked as though they had been bought from a North Street shop in Boston. Another thing I remember was his short bell crowned hat."

Founded in 1636 by a tough Puritan who later was badgered back to England because of his heretical writing, burned to the ground by Indians in 1675, Springfield now harbors in its metropolitan area more than half a million persons. It is the largest city in the Connecticut River Valley.

The Garand rifle was invented here in the U.S. Armory and Arsenal which sits on a site selected by George Washington. Beginning with the production of muskets in 1795, the Armory was manufacturing automatic weapons in 1968 when it was phased out. In 1864 more than 3,000 men worked there producing 1,000 rifles a day for the Union Army. The famous Springfield rifle was made there.

John Brown, the abolitionist, once lived there for two years, from 1847 to 1849, working sporadically as a wool merchant, more assiduously at operating an underground railway station assisting fugitive slaves escape into Canada.

Springfield, Massachusetts

Today Springfield and the small cities clustering about it on the river — Chicopee, Holyoke, Agawam, West Springfield — are fed by light industry, but the area is still weapons-oriented. Massive Westover Air Force Base, an SAC installation, is in its suburbs.

Springfield's power house

Chicopee

Looking northward from Mount Tom

Holyoke is the technicolor eyesore of the valley, with its ingenious three-canal system — linked to the finally successful dam at Hadley Falls — that uses river water three times, and also three times stains and taints it with dye and other industrial offal.

Near here, below Mount Tom, is the Great Oxbow — 200 acres of water — that surrounded the Mount Tom sawmill of the Connecticut Valley Lumber Company. Here in the oxbow's placid waters were boomed the pine and spruce and hemlock cut far upstream in Vermont and New Hampshire — on Indian Stream near the Canadian border, on Simms Stream and Paul Stream and on Peacham Hollow Brook.

All winter the loggers in two states cut the timber, hauled it to the margins of a hundred frozen streams, and piled it into giant rollways, waiting for ice-out and high water to float the logs to the sawmills. It was the longest log drive in the world. Some logs were driven the full length of the river, 410 miles to Long Island Sound.

But few went past Mount Tom. And none use the river as a sluice today. The last long logs were driven on it in 1915; the last pulpwood drive was in 1948. Once most of the timber cut in New Hampshire and Vermont used the river as a highway; today trucks haul it to the mills.

Holyoke and its canals, from the air

Northampton

The valley irons out here, flatter and flatter with mineral riches in its soil.

Some rivers are wildly beautiful in spots and then sludge through miles of drabness. Not so the Connecticut. It looks good almost everywhere. It is one of the most consistently beautiful rivers in the world.

At times, with run-off, it's the color of a wet deer hide, but even so,

> . . . still it sings the same sweet song
> And still it tells its tale.
> Complaining of commercial wrong
> To forest, hill and dale.
> It longs for freedom from the mills,
> To be forever free,
> To sweep unharnessed through the hills
> From cataract to sea.*

The poet was purple when he wrote that praise of the Connecticut seventy years ago, but the river evokes purple prose as easily as it generates electric power.

The Song of the River, by Joe Cone, *Connecticut Magazine*, Vol. 7, 1901

72

Near Hatfield

Some have said the valley is the most educated on the continent. Yale started at its mouth; and Wesleyan at Middletown remains near the river, as do Trinity and the University of Hartford and Smith and Amherst and Mount Holyoke and the University of Massachusetts and Deerfield Academy and the new Hampshire College and American International College at Springfield and then further north, Dartmouth College that started in Lebanon, Connecticut, and moved into the wilderness of New Hampshire because its president, Eleazar Wheelock, could no longer stand the complaints of Connecticut apple farmers that his students plucked the trees before the farmers could.

Not far from this spot at Sunderland, where the waters have regained some purity, the dumps dump in, the bright dye empties vomit-yellow into the stream, and sewers make their flushing periodic deposits.

The wonder is not so much that the dumps, the dye, the offal is sent into the river, but that the senders care so little about the beauty they are wasting. Their attitude is more astounding than their actions; can it really be that they care so little for their neighbors or think so little about them? Is it contempt or callousness or blindness?

74

Tobacco farms near Deerfield

Tobacco, but not the shade-grown, tender, long leaf used for cigar wrappers and grown under a rich mosaic of colored tenting, is native to the valley.

The Indians grew it, and it was the Indian men themselves who chopped out the weeds with crude hoes of wood or bone, although they did not shoulder their females out of the corn and pumpkin fields. Tobacco was too important and too sacred to be tended by women; other crops were not.

The Indians mixed the small round leaves with sumac to make pipe tobacco, and brewed a thin brown tobacco punch from it. The Puritans picked up the habit and soon passed regulations about tobacco drinking. By 1647 the Connecticut General Court had prohibited tobacco use to anyone under twenty-one, unless with a doctor's prescription. Teen-age addicts, however — those hooked with the habit before the anti-tobacco law was passed — were allowed to smoke it in their kitchens and parlors, but never in public.

Later, broadleaf Virginia tobacco was introduced and thrived in the fertile

Hinsdale, New Hampshire

valley. In 1801 Mrs. Prout of South Windsor began to sell "Long Nines," the first American cigar, and by 1820 East Windsor and Suffield were heavily into the cigar business, turning out hand-rolled Supers and Windsor Particulars, as well as Long Nines.

In 1901 Enfield introduced shade-grown tobacco and its production spread in both directions, ranging up the valley from Portland, Connecticut, to Greenfield, Massachusetts, more or less. But by 1950 a disease that scientists called "weather fleck" began to affect the plants. It is caused by a change in the weather of the valley — a change made by man with automobile exhaust and industrial chimney stack. Smog.

Bellows Falls, Vermont

By the time the traveler reaches upstream into Vermont, what has been simply a beautiful river now becomes spectacular. The valley narrows, squeezing out the flat, rich, lowland flood plains of Massachusetts, and pours the river's waters down between steep-rising hills, sometimes into gorges. As Henry Van Dyke has said about rivers and people, "The greatest are not always the most agreeable nor the best to live with."

The forest changes. The tobacco lands are left behind and the hardwoods become flecked with the year-round greenery of pine and spruce, and farther up the river, the valley's woods are dominated by dark green conifers.

The river roars at Bellows Falls, and it was here, fifty miles into Vermont, that the first attempts to bridge and harness it were made. In 1785 Colonel Enoch Hale built a covered bridge 365 feet long, with its planked roadway 50 feet above the river. This was the first bridge across the Connecticut and the only one until 1796, when a bridge was built downstream at Springfield, Massachusetts.

78

Colonel Hale's bridge was replaced in 1840 by Tucker's bridge, and this, although still strong, was replaced in 1930. Both early bridges had toll houses, and Hetty Howland Green, a direct descendant of the Howland who landed at Plymouth on the *Mayflower*, and one of the richest and tightest women in the world (her son's leg was amputated because she refused to pay for medical attention, trying again and again, dressed in rags, to get free doctoring) is supposed to have collected toll on Tucker's bridge.

A bronze plaque near the bridge tells of "The Bellows Falls Canal. Here the first canal in the U.S. was built in 1802. The British-owned company, which was chartered to render the Connecticut River navigable here in 1791, was ten years building the nine locks and dam around the Great Falls, 52 feet high. After the railroad came in 1849, river traffic declined and the canal was used for water power only."

Once, during a long-log drive on the river in the early part of this century, a logger tending out with a pike pole slipped at the sluice high above the falls. His pike pole was swept fifty feet below into the spume, but he caught an iron peg in the concrete and finally pulled himself back up to the log boom. He stared long at the foot of the dam where the logs thundered down. A fellow logger shouted, "You figger on going back down there?"

"No, by God," he replied. "I'm just looking at my fingerprints on that iron."

Not far upstream from here at Brattleboro, Vermont, is where the first United States postage stamps were made and issued by the town postmaster in 1845 and 1846.

Rudyard Kipling, who married a Brattleboro girl, lived there for several years until 1896. *Captains Courageous*, the *Jungle Books*, and the *Just So Stories* were written there. He left after — and perhaps because of — discovering a peculiarity in local banking habits. He had been always irritated when his small checks made out for a few dollars to the grocer or butcher were never cashed; he never felt secure in balancing his check book. But he was infuriated when he discovered that Brattleboro merchants were selling his checks to collectors — as autographs — at considerably more than they were made out for.

Bellows Falls, the town

Here now the river is owned by New Hampshire. Vermont owns a nibbling bite of the west shore above low-water mark, but the bed of the Connecticut — its sand and rolling rock and ice-scarred granite at the ledges of its falls — is all New Hampshire. You must have a New Hampshire fishing license to flick a fly into the Connecticut, and New Hampshire pockets the license fee. On the other hand, New Hampshire must maintain the bridges, a frugal fact that sours a New Hampshireman and delights a Vermonter.

Since colonial times the upper valley towns had quarreled about where the boundary was. At one time some New Hampshire townsmen wanted to become Vermonters by moving the boundary east into New Hampshire instead of moving themselves west into Vermont. For years New Hampshire had both historical and monetary claims to the river as its own. Long before the name Vermont was coined, land between the river and the Green Mountains was called the New Hampshire Grants; in 1791, in order to become the fourteenth state, Vermont agreed upon the west bank as its boundary with New Hampshire, and in addition, New Hampshire had been building the Connecticut River bridges linking it with Vermont. But in about 1915 Vermont, knowing that power dams to be built along the river would be wonderfully taxable, brought about legal action that was settled in 1933 by the Supreme Court of the United States. New Hampshire won, and more than one hundred boundary monuments and markers stand on the Vermont side — some of them 6½ feet of granite embedded safely above high water and surging ice lines, 1200 pounds for each of them, indicating where the true line is.

As the dams were built, both New Hampshire and Vermont towns taxed the power companies for the land the companies occupied. It resulted in a standstill. Both states (through their towns) get about $2 million annually from the dam sites.

Now each seven years the attorneys general of each state, or their representatives, perambulate the boundary line to be sure the markers are still there and that New Hampshire has not moved into Vermont or vice versa.

Perhaps the boundary disputes were the basis for the up-country story of the Connecticut River Valley farmer who was told that his farm, as a result of a survey, was really in New Hampshire, instead of in Vermont as he'd always thought. "Thank God," he said. "I didn't think I could stand another of those Vermont winters."

The New England covered bridge was not built for kissing couples to hide in, or for keeping snow off the planking of the bridge. In fact, each winter the selectmen, in horse-and-sleigh times, hired men to haul snow into the bridges and spread it out so that sleighs could travel through more easily.

Covered bridges were covered to protect the wooden trusses from the weather. It was the crossed truss that made the bridge so strong, that allowed it, in pre-I-beam times, to span such great distances, and that truss needed to be saved from rot.

The Windsor covered bridge, the longest in the nation, is one of five covered bridges crossing the Connecticut. (All are in New Hampshire because the river is owned by New Hampshire.) Others are farther north — at Columbia, Haverhill, Lancaster, and Pittsburg.

The Windsor bridge is two spans stretching 460 feet across the river, supported by a stone pier with pointed, upstream cutwaters to protect it from being battered down by ice and log drives. First built in 1796, it was destroyed by floods in 1824, 1848, and 1866. Once it was a privately owned toll bridge. Since being rebuilt by Bela Fletcher and James Tasker after the 1866 flood, it has been altered only once, in 1954, when it was strengthened by the state of New Hampshire.

Just south of here in Colonial days there was a "mast camp" where royal foresters gathered the giant pines that had been marked with the King's arrow and reserved for the crown, to become masts in the King's navy.

Near White River Junction, Vermont

Sawmill slash and sawdust and wooden crating are all organic. Unlike glass, aluminum, or plastic, they will in time mush themselves back into compost and feed living things again. But at a river's edge, they slough off into the water, rob it of oxygen needed by fish. They need not be here, a blotch on a beautiful river, so near to where boys canoe downstream in a manhood ritual, learning about themselves, about nature, and about other men who build sawmills on a river's bank.

Canoe trip on the upper river

Farther downstream — at Springfield, Holyoke, and Hartford — the river's banks are busy banks, industrious and active. But in the reaches of New Hampshire and Vermont, it seems the river is not much concerned with such. Here the river is little involved with today or tomorrow, but it has much yesterday.

Here at Orford Samuel Morey chugged back and forth across the river in 1793 in his little steamboat, the *Aunt Sally*, fourteen years before Robert Fulton, famed for inventing the steamboat, launched his *Clermont*. Morey, who had shown Fulton his own steamboat, was furious with Fulton, accused him of theft (although Morey had not patented his own boat), and in pique sank the *Aunt Sally* in nearby Lake Morey.

A little south of here, at Hanover, New Hampshire, John Ledyard, a twenty-one-year-old student from Groton, Connecticut, became one of Dartmouth College's first dropouts when in May of 1773 he hacked out a dugout (supposedly 50 feet long) from a pine log and floated down the Connecticut 150 miles or more to Hartford. With a bearskin for warmth, and volumes of Ovid and a Greek testament for amusement, he nearly drifted over Bellows Falls, but paddled ashore in time, and got oxen to drag his dugout around the falls.

He seems to have kept going from momentum. He later sailed with Cook on his third voyage around the world. He explored the Pacific Northwest, and like an arctic Marco Polo, walked the breadth of Siberia.

"In all my travels in this country and Europe I have never seen any village more beautiful than this," Washington Irving wrote of Orford, New Hampshire.

The town has, side by side, in what is called Bulfinch Row, seven of the most incredibly beautiful houses in the valley. One of them may have been designed by Charles Bulfinch (1763–1844), one of the nation's early architects. The others supposedly were inspired by the graceful, spacious lines of the first house and were patterned after it.

North of Orford it becomes even more beautiful. The valley surpasses itself, and Vermont seems greener than New Hampshire despite its being simply one of two slopes draining into the stream at their bottom junction. Yet it is true. The Vermont side indeed is greener. The glacier scraped much more harshly at New Hampshire's peaks, leaving them raw stone, fleshless for these thousands of years, rude, white-gleaming in the summer sun, white-snow-covered in the winter.

Then too, a hundred years and more ago, New Hampshire went industrial while Vermont stayed with the cow, saying that it preferred it so. Therefore, New Hampshire's light-green tender meadows and its fields of hay are now the darker green of forest in a once-was field. You can't see far through forest, but Vermont's vistas are made possible by grazing cows and the chattering sickle-bar blades of a mowing machine that not only clean-cuts the hay, but also severs new popple seedlings from their roots soon after they seed into the field. In New England, fields are forests thwarted.

Now here — with the land so clean and clear, with problems simple ones of breed and bread and barn and bairn — now here we can see why both New Hampshire men and Vermonters are inconstant conservationists.

Look. And smell. Breathe deeply. Feel the air; touch it now and sense its purity, its vigor, its super-constant juvenation (that supposedly has given Vermonters their long life — if you discount their stubbornness). Suck in the honest pine scent, the pure (yet cough-producing) woodstove woodsmoke, the honeysuckle spring, the wild violet, the skunk cabbage. Suck this in and try to understand that mass-breeding is a threat. It seems impossible.

Look around. Look to the hills and the streams splashing to the valleys. Indeed there are more cows than people — a highly desirable ratio.

And so how can you feel a threat of population pollution? It makes no sense in these hills, along this valley, and this problem must be other men's in other places, and those overpopulated men cannot ever reach this place — not ever.

Why spend fool's time and effort to save what needs no saving? Who can contaminate this huge, clean, rain-drenched, sun-scoured, tree-protected land?

We can.

Timothy Dwight, Yale president from 1795 for twenty years and one of the most traveled of nineteenth-century Americans, wrote of the Connecticut: "This stream may perhaps with more propriety than any other in the world be named the beautiful river. From Stuart [Stewartstown, New Hampshire] to the Sound [about four hundred miles] it uniformly maintains this character. The purity, salubrity and sweetness of its waters; the frequency and elegance of its meanders; its absolute freedom from all aquatic vegetables; the uncommon and universal beauty of its banks, here a smooth and winding beach, there covered with rich verdure, now fringed with bushes, now covered with lofty trees, and now formed by the intruding hill, the rude bluff and the shaggy mountain — are objects which no traveler can thoroughly describe."

Upstream it's changed so little (although there are some local eyesores) — the downstream blotches of Hartford, Holyoke, Springfield — these are really very little — and so correctible.

96

Another wonderful river story — and probably as apocryphal as the one about the Indentured Servants' League Against Eating Salmon — concerns a logger named Ed Smith (he's always Ed Smith in all the versions) who dropped off in Woodsville, New Hampshire, during a spring river drive for a little relaxation in the town.

After a tour of the local saloons, he caught sight of a department store dummy, dressed in women's underclothing, in the show window of Sargent's store. Unable to resist her appeal, he whooped a mighty rutting call and leaped right through the plate glass window to ravish the dummy as he held it.

He was arrested, of course, jailed, of course; and all versions of the story have him drowned on the drive the following spring — at Perry Falls, or Fifteen-Mile Falls, or First Lake.

Woodsville was a lusty town, not only because the log drives of the Connecticut, the Ammonoosuc, and the Wells met there, but also because it was a railroad center. But besides its saloons and red-light houses, it also had its pride. A thoughtful Woodsville man once wrote, "Woodsville is the doughnut; Wells River is the hole," the sort of solemn pronouncement not designed to please the Vermonters in Wells River across the Connecticut.

As early as 1812 Woodsville was a busy river town with as many as fourteen river boats tied up there at one time, bound for Hartford with cargoes of shingles, hides, ashes, potash, and lumber. The river boats had one mast and a square sail, and when there was wind the crew could rest, but otherwise they used the "white-ash breeze" — long poles that reached to the river bottom. Upstream they brought sugar, iron, molasses, salt, grindstones, rum — and perhaps plate glass windows.

Wells River, Vermont

Wells River

McIndoes Falls Dam, near Monroe, New Hampshire

A good river man, the oldtime loggers used to say, could "throw a piece of soap into the water and ride the bubbles to shore."

But that was before the dams cut off the log drives. That was before McIndoes Dam and Moore Dam turned Fifteen-Mile Falls (really more like twenty miles long) into two long lakes and buried the rapids under a hundred feet of water.

But before those thousands of tons of concrete stuffed shut the rapids, men rode bateaus down the falls, chasing logs, demonstrating their superior manhood, and often dying for their foolhardiness. They were buried in pork barrels wearing their calked boots, usually not far from where they drowned. In 1930 construction men building the dam at McIndoes dug up several of those old burial barrels at the foot of Mulliken's Pitch, one of the most dangerous spots on the river. The calked boots seemed still usable.

Monroe

Robert E. Pike, in his *Tall Trees, Tough Men*, shows what the river once was in a logger's ballad at least fifty years old:

> The ice is black and rotten and the
>   rollways are piled high
> So boost upon your peavey sticks
>   while I do tell you why.
>
> . . .
>
> All the gutters run with whiskey
>   when the shanty boys so frisky.
> Set their boot calks in the sidewalks
>   when the drive is down
>
> . . .
>
> But break the rollways out, my lads, and
>   let the big sticks slide
> For one man killed within the woods,
>   ten's drownded on the drive.

Barnet's main claim to fame is something that never happened to her in 1826. It was supposed to, but by some calculation gone awry, by some message gone askew, the target was missed by more than a hundred miles.

Barnet, Vermont, was the head of navigation on the river. Flatboats, similar to those tied up downstream at Woodsville, docked there regularly, but there were great plans to push past Barnet, to build a canal around the Fifteen-Mile Falls and to link with other yet-unbuilt canals that would eventually connect with the St. Lawrence.

True, the dream canals were not yet there, but it was time for a real steam-boat, instead of merely flatboats, to reach up to Barnet. So a 70-foot sternwheeler was christened the *Barnet* in New York City and headed north. She was 14½ feet wide, drew about 2 feet of water loaded, and was powered by two 20–hp steam engines. On a clear day, without too thick a fog to buck against, she could make about five miles an hour going upstream in slow water.

Of his trip on a similar boat on the Connecticut, Dickens wrote, "... we all kept in the middle of the deck lest it unexpectedly tip over. The machinery worked between the deck and the keel; the whole forming a warm sandwich about three feet thick."

The *Barnet* steamed up through the Enfield Rapids in high water, for the Windsor Locks Canal was not yet finished. At the Willimansett Rapids near Spring-field, men waded into the river to grab lines and pull her over the falls. At Brattleboro, Vermont, most of the town got drunk when she whistled in.

Next morning she headed north with twenty-five miles to go to Bellows Falls. She fetched up on a sandbar and oxen pulled her off. Then Bellows Falls itself. She tied up below the falls and the crew went ashore to celebrate. Thirty-one speeches were made at a banquet in her honor that night.

On the following day she steamed up to the first of the canal locks, stopped a while, and then steamed back downstream. She was too fat to fit. Barnet was to do without the *Barnet;* Hartford got her.

Barnet, Vermont

Thank God for farmers. Many of them have made the land even more beautiful than nature did; they've improved it.

So much of what is left for us to love about the river is there because of the farmer's strong reluctance to tamper with the tides of nature. A farmer — Yankee or Nebraskan or Yorkshireman or Pole — has an enormous innate need to simply hold still, to keep what he's got, to limit his greed to what he can keep. He wants control. What's the use of owning more than you can plough, or hay, or cut into sawlogs or pulp or firewood in wintertime, or drive spiles into to bleed out maple sap in sugar time? No use, at all. In the Connecticut Valley, this Yankee trait has saved a lot of beauty.

Then too, since the nineteenth century when a million or more fine Spanish-bred Merino sheep close-grazed the valley, poverty has set in. The farmers let the fields go fallow, and the woods — first the "popples," then the birch and sumac and wild cherry — seeded themselves into the fields. Later they were succeeded by pines and spruce which strangled the early field invaders. This was reclamation poverty. Many an upcountry Connecticut Valley farm was conserved by nature because the farmer could not afford to be a farmer any longer.

"Leave it as it is," wrote Theodore Roosevelt. "The ages have been at work on it, and man can only mar it." Yet each year I–91 creeps farther up the river, its four lanes of concrete reaching deeper into what should be left as it is.

Now New Haven is 184 miles (70-miles-per-hour miles, perhaps two and a half hours) away from Norwich, Vermont, along some of the most breath-takingly beautiful highway and riverscape in the world.

Each year it ribbons farther north, and by 1977 New York, New Jersey, and Connecticut cars will be able to jolt into St. Johnsbury, Vermont, at about the rate of a superfast automated double Detroit assembly line. And as steadily.

Worse, I–93 from New Hampshire and from such lower spots as Lowell, Lawrence, and sweaty Boston will have been married to I–91 south of St. Johnsbury after crossing the river near Moore Dam, and New England will have been tilted to drain its auto sludge north across New Hampshire and taint the brooks with hydrocarbon fuel stains, and film the firs with petroleum fumes, and strew the verge with bottles and beer cans, candy wrappers and car-tossed garbage.

The happy shrieks of city children in the wilderness do not compensate for this.

But again, those who live near Moore Dam now and breathe clean air as if it were a right because they always have — they know how much room they have. Lots.

And who could believe — especially such Vermonters and New Hampshire-men along such a wondrous river — that Americans fleeing crowded Manhattan would really indeed and honestly drive north two hundred miles or more in a spawning surge to crowd yet another reef in a spasm of escape? To duplicate Manhattan in Vermont? To legislate, by increasing population, a Levittown in the leafmold of the White Mountains?

Absurd, of course. Yet the Kennebunk slums — stretching thirty ugly miles along the sea from Kittery to Portland, Maine — were made by men who loved the land, and wanted to escape more southern city slums. They loved the land too well.

On a roadside near Moore Dam

Moore Dam, from the air

Moore Reservoir, near Littleton, New Hampshire

Gilman, Vermont

Near Gilman, looking northward

Here the river's in no hurry; nor are the people on its banks. They're as peaceful as the land around them, as passive, and as permanent.

In the area of Lancaster, New Hampshire, the river drops only two feet in ten miles, and the meanders twist in the nearly level valley, doubling back on themselves in tranquil certitude, looking backward as much as forward. Perhaps it's pleased with its solidity and conservatism, calm, unrushed, unrestless in its dalliance.

An oxbow such as this is so serpentine that a man standing in New Hampshire can fire a rifle west and his bullet will cross both Vermont and New Hampshire before lodging in Vermont soil half a mile away.

Lancaster, winter

Lancaster, covered bridge

The woods, uncut, will not support a man in any fiscal sense. But wood cut down makes work, and factories, and paper. Man needs all. And in northern New Hampshire, in such places as Groveton where this paper mill is a major employer, the valley men are often short of work. They cling there still, however, and even their youth do not want to leave as youth almost always does. Despite nearly chronic hard times, they stay to reap the valley's loveliness, as their ancestors once reaped the valley's mowings.

But making paper, and making jobs, does not mean that fish must die. There is no blood vendetta between river fish and papermakers. Fish can live and man can thrive. These indeed are quite compatible. No more belly-up from acid water.

118

Groveton, paper mill

Groveton, some casualties

Colebrook

Near Colebrook

North of here for nearly ninety miles the river's free of contamination, itself as sweet as Benét's "little sweet-tasting brooks of the blond country."

Here are clean bright glory and the rainbow, squaretail, and brown trout that must have such purity, or die.

This is the country of Albert "Jigger" Johnson, the famous woods boss who declared that he could "run faster, jump higher, squat lower, move sideways quicker, and spit further than any son-of-a-bitch in camp." And no one ever challenged him. They knew he could, and more.

It's the country of Long Tom Currier, who always recorded his height as 5 feet 16 inches — and was accurate. This is the home of the giant Magalloway hare, which has never been seen but often heard and which has supernatural abilities, especially with hunting guides filled with evening whiskey around a camp woodstove.

Upcountry, the thinning land

But even here with so much pure, untouched land growing clean black spruce in perfect cones, owned in such huge quantities by the state and by paper and power companies, the wooden necklaces of cottages are beginning to strangle the small lakes. Perhaps it's *because* so much land is not on the summer-people market; perhaps the huge ownership is saving it — a thesis much more evident. But the signs say Lots for Sale and the wells will be sunk and the septic systems dug and people will squat there for the summer months.

First Connecticut Lake

A dam creates Lake Francis as the river dwindles down, and there are others at the lower ends of both First and Second Connecticut Lakes.

But the other lakes, Third Lake and Fourth — large ponds, really — are free of restraint; at least of man's restraint. But they still obey the laws of gravity and erosion and evaporation, and diminishing source.

There are orange daisies in these meadows and black-eyed Susans, and in the

The narrow channel between lakes

Second Connecticut Lake, the dam

Second Connecticut Lake.

wintertime there is more snow than a man knows what to do with. So he does little with it except to push it around the roads a bit and rest up until spring.

First Connecticut Lake has an annual snowfall of more than 172 inches. That's more than fourteen feet, somewhat higher than "crotch-deep on a nine-foot Indian," which is one upcountry measurement of small snowfalls. Mount Washington, sixty miles to the south, with some of the most severe winter weather on the continent, has only 200 inches of snow annually.

Third Connecticut Lake

There's a man who sells land around a pond near here. He says it's great for summer people, especially when it's only seven hours to Boston and "six hours is coming up fast."

It is. It is great. The Connecticut River is an infant brook not far from here, so narrow you can straddle it. You can cup it in your hand and sip its sweetness.

The man's right, too, about the trip. Seven hours now. Six hours coming up fast. That isn't too much time.

Headwater stream, winter

132

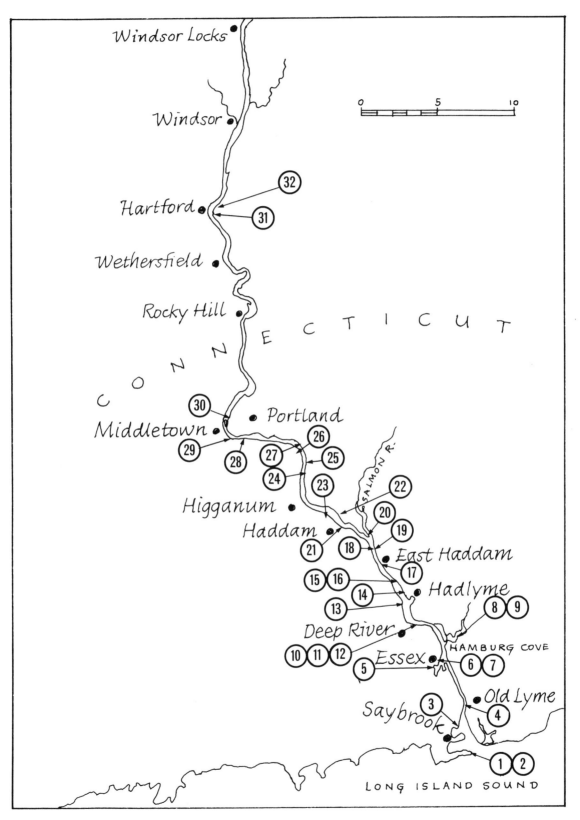

Map I. From Long Island Sound to Windsor Locks

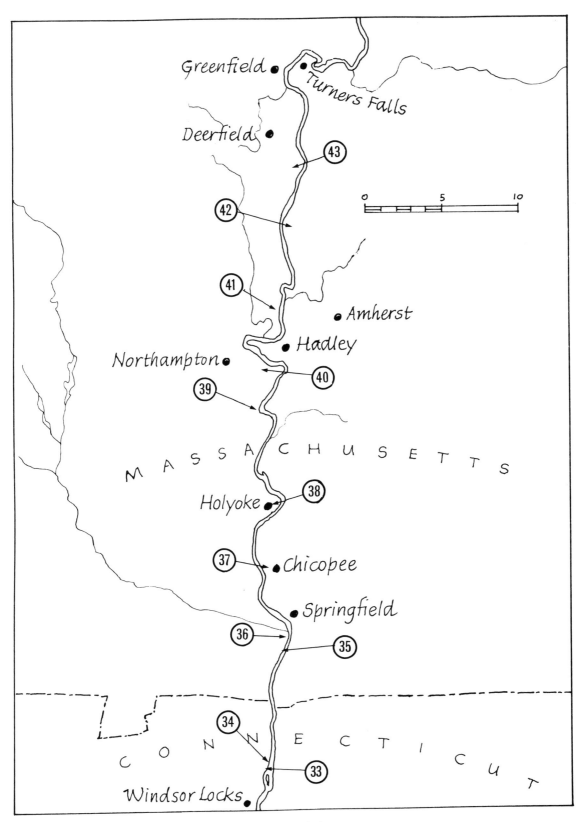

Map II. From Windsor Locks to Greenfield's vicinity

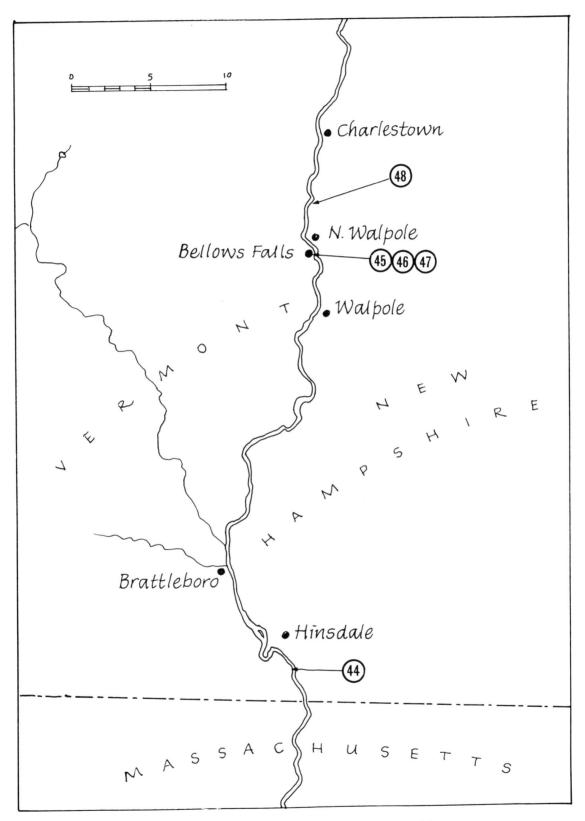

Map III. From Greenfield's vicinity to Charlestown, New Hampshire

138

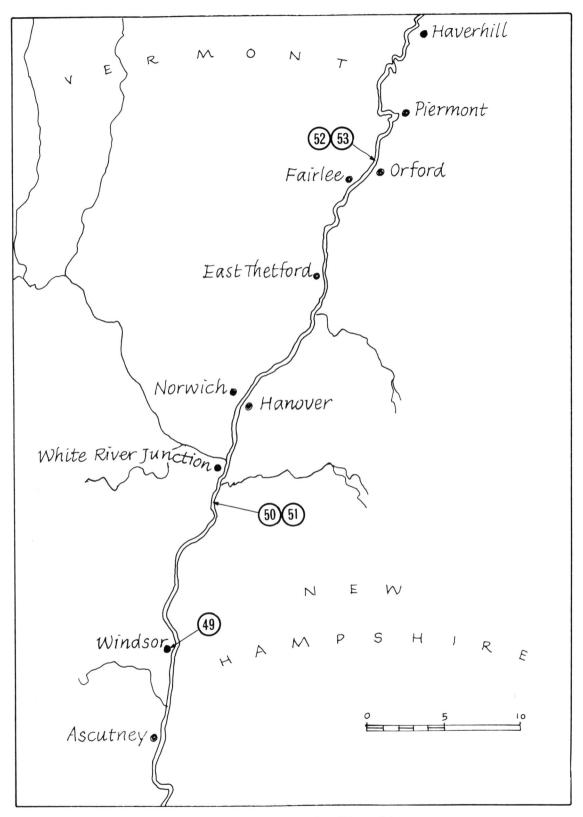

Map IV. From Ascutney, Vermont, to Haverhill, New Hampshire

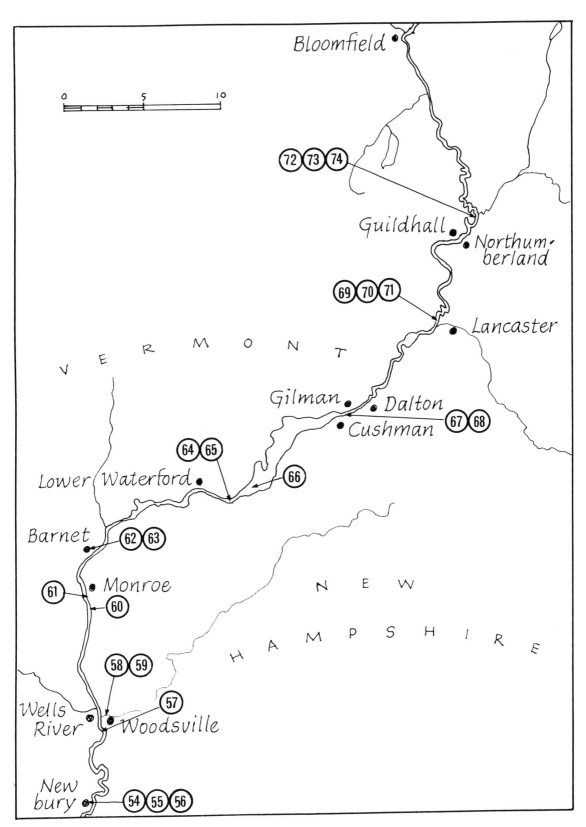

Map V. From Newbury, Vermont, to Bloomfield, Vermont

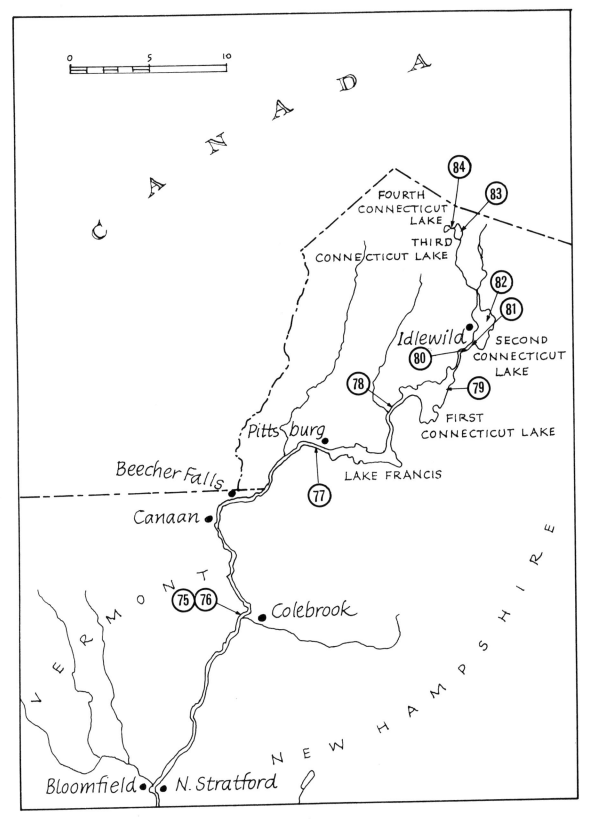

Map VI. From Bloomfield, Vermont, to the headwaters